The Primary Comprehension Toolkit

Lessons

In the Toolkit, we emphasize reading to explore and learn about the world.

In this Strategy Book, the lessons for summarizing and synthesizing are:

Strategy Support

firsthand
HEINEMANN
DEDICATED TO TEACHERS™

Copyright 2008 by Stephanie Harvey and Anne Goudvis. All rights reserved.

The authors and publisher wish to thank those who have generously given permission to reprint borrowed materials.

Strategy Book 6:
Summarize and Synthesize

Synthesizing information nudges readers to see the bigger picture, pull together their thinking, and organize their learning to share it with others. It's not enough for readers to simply recall or restate the facts—they use a variety of comprehension strategies including asking questions, inferring, and determining what's important to understand big ideas. We begin by simply asking young readers to stop and collect their thoughts before reading on. We give kids time, materials, and support to use comprehension strategies as tools for investigating curriculum-related and self-selected topics. Children summarize and synthesize their thinking through creating poems, posters, books, and other projects that demonstrate their learning and understanding.

In this Strategy Book, we demonstrate how we use comprehension strategies to teach content and do research. Here kids apply reading and thinking strategies to delve deeply into a social studies/science topic. Once kids understand how to learn new information, ask questions, and make connections and inferences, as well as interact with each other and work collaboratively, they are ready to use strategies as tools for learning. In this group of lessons, kids build their knowledge about and research the rain forest. However, these lessons on the research process work with any topic, either a curriculum-related one or topics kids choose to investigate on their own.

D0503412

Library of Congress Cataloging-in-Publication Data
CIP data on file with the Library of Congress

Summarize and Synthesize
ISBN-13: 978-0-325-02153-9
ISBN-10: 0-325-02153-8

Primary Comprehension Toolkit: Language and Lessons for Active Literacy
ISBN-13: 978-0-325-00997-1
ISBN-10: 0-325-00997-X

Printed in the United States of America on acid-free paper

13   ML   5

Summarize
Information

Text Matters

As kids tackle ways to summarize information, we choose texts that have just enough information so that kids can absorb and write about it without getting bogged down in TMI—too much information. Articles with subheadings and distinct sections are perfect for kids just learning to summarize: they can use just a paragraph or section of the text. Before writing a summary, we confer with kids to make sure they have understood what they are reading, recorded the information accurately, and put the information in their own words.

Resources & Materials

Lesson Text

TIME For Kids Bigger Picture Edition [Spring 2003] "Welcome to the Rain Forest" poster

Additional Texts

A variety of books and magazines about the rain forest and other topics

Classroom Supplies

- *How Do We Create a Summary?* Anchor Chart
- Post-its, markers, and chart paper

Student Supplies

- Post-its and notes written previously, either by kids or the teacher
- Post-its, paper and markers, pencils, and crayons

Put it in your own words and keep it interesting

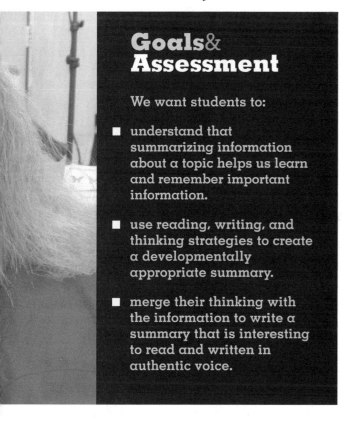

Goals& Assessment

We want students to:

- understand that summarizing information about a topic helps us learn and remember important information.

- use reading, writing, and thinking strategies to create a developmentally appropriate summary.

- merge their thinking with the information to write a summary that is interesting to read and written in authentic voice.

Why&What

Summaries run the gamut—they can be oral, written, or drawn! In this lesson, we teach kids who already have information and notes on a topic to transform them into a summary. Depending on children's reading and writing development, summaries can look very different. An emergent reader and writer may draw a picture and jot down a sentence or two. A more developed reader may summarize learning in a complete paragraph. During the lesson we first create a summary of the *TFK* "Welcome to the Rain Forest" poster based on information kids share orally. Then we convene a small group to sort and organize notes that kids have written previously. They organize their Post-its to put their ideas in order and create a summary paragraph. Whatever form a summary takes, we make sure kids' enthusiasm and authentic voices don't get lost as they write up what they've learned.

How

Connect and Engage

- Discuss: What is a *summary* and what is a *topic*?
- Review information kids have learned from reading and taking notes on a topic.
- Explain summary writing.
- Explain note-taking.

Model

- Explain how to combine information and thinking on a topic to create a group summary.
- Start with important information and demonstrate how to organize it.
- Show how adding questions and thoughts merges thinking with the information.

Guide

- Share an Anchor Chart that lists the steps of writing a summary.

Collaborate or Practice Independently

- Pull a small group together to create a summary with information they have already gathered while the rest of the class works individually or in pairs.
- Check to see that the gathered information is in kids' own words and is accurate.
- Think about the topic and then organize and combine the information from Post-its to make sentences.
- Respond to kids' individual needs as they read, take notes, and organize information.
- Confer with children to correct misconceptions.

Share the Learning

- Have kids share summaries to wrap up the lesson.

Used with permission from *Time For Kids*.

Lesson Text

The "Welcome to the Rain Forest" poster is perfect for teaching kids to write a summary—moving from their notes to sentences—because it contains a manageable amount of lively information. Organizing the information kids have learned about the rain forest canopy provides an opportunity to talk through information and launch into writing. When kids include their reactions, responses, and illustrations, a summary of the text comes to life!

TEACHING MOVES   **TEACHING LANGUAGE**

Connect and Engage

Discuss: What is a *summary* and what is a *topic*?

Today we'll try something new—writing a *summary!* A summary pulls together what we know about a topic so we can share the information with others. A summary is often a paragraph in which all the sentences relate to one topic. A *topic* is what we are reading and thinking about. You can often tell what the topic is from the title. Let's look at the title, "Welcome to the Rain Forest." What's the topic?

[Kids shout out.] The rain forest!

Review information kids have learned from reading and taking notes on a topic.

Exactly. Let's review some of the information we learned from the *TFK* article "Welcome to the Rain Forest." All the information relates to the topic: life in the rain forest canopy. The canopy is a habitat made up of the leaves and branches of all those big trees. It's what the article calls the "forest roof," and the animals spend much of their life in the trees rather than on the ground. All these animals are adapted to living in these trees—in the rain forest canopy. We'll focus on the animals in the canopy for our topic. Most of you have written notes or Post-its about them. Now let's turn and talk about what you learned about these animals. *[I write the information on an Anchor Chart.]*

TIP: Writing the information kids share in phrases makes it easier and quicker to record it.

Adolfo: I learned that the little blue frog is really poisonous and dangerous! Its color tells animals to stay away from it.

Gerald: Wow! I didn't know that the sloth carries its babies on its belly!

Zoe: That horned katydid—that scary-looking insect—has spikes on its body to protect itself. It comes out at night.

Joshua: Oh boy, I'd hate to step on that insect!

TEACHING LANGUAGE	TEACHING MOVES

You have such interesting information about our topic: the animals that live in the rain forest canopy. When we write a summary, we write what is important about the topic in our own words. We'll use all this great information to write a summary of animals that live in the canopy.

Explain summary writing.

Anything else that we should add to our notes?

Citlalli: I went online and read that the blue frog eats poisonous ants. When it eats these ants, its skin gets full of poison, so animals can't even touch it!

Good for you, Citlalli! You did some research.

Tanika: Sloths spend hours hanging upside down in the trees. They are really strange-looking animals!

Adolpho: I'm amazed that some animals spend their whole life up in the trees.

I think we're going to take the information you just shared orally and see if we can shape this information into new thoughts to make a summary. Notice that I wrote notes on the chart using just a few words, not whole sentences, and that I paraphrased the information. We'll turn these words and phrases into sentences as we write our summary.

Explain note-taking.

what we Learned about
The Rain Forest Canopy

- blue frog - poisonous and dangerous

- color tells animals to stay away from it

- sloth carries babies on its belly

- horned Katydid - has spikes for protection

- blue frog - gets its poison from poisonous ants

- sloths - hang upside down, strange looking!

TIP: Taking notes in words and phrases is an acquired skill. We work so hard to teach kids to write in complete sentences that writing a phrase can be tough at first! But we show kids how to do this because it is more efficient and they are less likely to parrot the text if they take notes in words and phrases, not sentences.

Model

You all mentioned interesting facts about the rain forest animals we learned about in the article. The information is accurate because we read it in the text and you put it into your own words when you shared it just now. Let's think about how we'll start our summary.

Notice the topic is about animals that live in the canopy, so we should talk about that first. I'll use what Adolfo said, that these are animals that spend their lives in trees! This is a big idea about the rain forest canopy. I'll write *The rain forest canopy is bursting with unusual, interesting animals that spend their lives in the leafy trees.* We try to use language that gets our reader interested in reading our summary, so I used the word *bursting.* The article didn't say that, but I know the rain forest canopy supports lots and lots of animals, so this is accurate information.

Start with important information and demonstrate how to organize it.

Now let's talk about the sloth.

Tanika: Let's say, "The sloth is a strange-looking animal that hangs upside down, holding onto tree branches with its claws. We were surprised it carries its babies on its belly!"

TIP: It does take some time for me to transcribe these long, detailed sentences, but as they watch and listen, kids can really internalize my modeling.

Good idea, Tanika, I'll add that. *[I write what Tanika says on the chart.]* What animal should we write about next?

Adolfo: Maybe the blue poison frog...that's a pretty weird frog.

OK, let's say *The blue poison frog is little but really dangerous. It is bright blue so animals know stay to away from it.* Notice that we are putting the information into our own words.

And then the katydid...we could say, "Another animal that looks really dangerous is the horned katydid—it has spikes that protect it." And finally let's wrap up the summary with a comment about all these animals. When we wrap up our summary, we want to end with our own thought. I think that animals in the canopy are amazing. So I'll write *You never know what kind of amazing animals you'll see in the rain forest canopy!*

Show how adding questions and thoughts merges thinking with the information.

Summary: Animals That Live in the Rain Forest Canopy

The rain forest canopy is bursting with unusual, interesting animals that spend their lives in the leafy trees. The sloth is a strange-looking animal that hangs upside down, holding on to tree branches with its claws. We were surprised that it carries its babies on its belly. The blue poison frog is little but really dangerous. It is bright blue so animals know to stay away from it. Another animal that looks really dangerous is the horned katydid—it has spikes that protect it. You never know what kind of amazing animals you'll see in the rain forest canopy!

Guide

[I share an Anchor Chart that I created prior to the lesson about how to create a summary. It will guide kids as they try this on their own, with a partner, or in a small group.]

Here's a list of what we do when writing a summary. Let's read it together. *[I read* How to Create a Summary *Anchor Chart.]* You can look at the chart for guidance as you try this yourself.

Share an Anchor Chart that lists the steps of writing a summary.

How to Create a Summary

1. Reread your notes on the topic. Make sure they are accurate and in your own words.

2. Think about the topic and the information that tells about it.

3. Put the notes in order—what comes first, second, third, etc.

4. Remember to tell what is important, but don't tell too much.

TIP: When concepts are sophisticated, we often create a chart ahead of time in order to give our undivided attention to teaching during the lesson. Then we can read and review the steps we just used to write our summary using the kids' oral information. We continue to use it throughout the lesson to guide summary writing. And kids who are writing summaries on their own can refer to it again and again.

Now you can go off to read, think, and take notes on Post-its. Work with a partner if you like. I will be working with small groups for awhile. You are welcome to try writing a summary on your own. Remember to tell important information—but don't tell too much.

TIP: We always check in with individuals to make sure they have a plan for working independently before we sit down with a small group.

Collaborate or Practice Independently

[I gather a small group of children who have Post-its of information about the TFK poster.]

Let's get started writing another summary together. Look over the Post-its you have and then turn and talk about them. *[After kids share their information with each other, I bring the group back together.]*

Let's see what we have. Who wants to share their information?

Johanna: I have a lot about the blue poison frog.

Joey: Me, too. I learned there are very, very blue frogs. They are poisonous!

Marisol: I learned that blue frogs give us a warning.

Johanna: The blue color tells animals to stay away.

Hold on! This is a lot of great information. Let's put our Post-its up so we can see them. *[I put kids' Post-its, detailing the information the kids have just shared, up on a the* Frog Information *chart (see page 8).]* We can use the information on these Post-its to write a summary about the blue poison frog.

Pull a small group together to create a summary with information they have already gathered while the rest of the class works individually or in pairs.

TIP: It makes sense to practice summarizing information in small groups, so that kids can participate more fully in the process. Meanwhile, the rest of the kids are pursuing more information by reading and taking notes on Post-its or thinksheets. Some kids may want to have a go at writing a summary on their own.

Check to see that the gathered information is in kids' own words and is accurate.

Think about the topic and then organize and combine the information from Post-its to make sentences.

[I point to the How to Create a Summary *Anchor Chart (see page 7). We review the steps on the chart.]* We notice that the first thing we do is to make sure our notes are in our own words and are accurate.

Now let's think about our topic—the blue frog. Think about what information we could start with. Turn and talk about these Post-its on the *Frog Information* chart. Let's see what makes the best first sentence. *[Kids turn and talk. Then I ask them to share.]*

Marisol: They are really poisonous—and really blue! Joey's Post-it says that.

Can you read it to us, Joey?

Joey: "I learned that there are very, very blue frogs. They are poisonous!"

Joey has already written his information in sentences. I'll start by writing his thought on our *Poisonous Blue Frog Summary* Anchor Chart. *[I write* We

TIP: The Post-it notes kids have already written guide our writing, but we discuss the information to make our writing more engaging. We also include the oral information kids share, which adds "voice" to our writing.

learned that there are very, very blue frogs and they are poisonous.] Let's look at our next step. Now we have to put the information on our Post-its in order. What comes next? Here's some information that relates to the poison. It's what you said, Marisol—that "blue frogs give us a warning." That explains the blue color we just wrote about. I'll write *The blue frog's bright color is a warning.*

> Johanna: Yeah, it says "Stay away from me! I'm poisonous!"

That is such a good idea, Johanna. That sounds a lot like your Post-it—except you just said it in a more interesting way. We want our summary to be interesting so people will read and learn from it. I'll write what you said. *[I write:* Stay away from me! I'm poisonous!*]*

Let's add some of our own thinking here. The blue frog's color means that it's poisonous and dangerous, so animals don't eat it. Here's where we could add Citlalli's information—it wasn't in the *TFK* poster, but she read it in another source. Remember, she said that the blue frog eats poisonous ants and this makes its skin poisonous. Totally amazing! How can I write that?

> Citlalli: Say "We were amazed to learn that blue frogs eat poisonous ants and their skin becomes poisonous!"

OK, and then let's end the summary by saying, "So don't touch those bright blue frogs!" Great job! You really took your information and shaped it into some new thoughts. Now we can share our paragraph, this summary, with other people and teach them about the blue poison frog.

Let's do some illustrations now because they will make our information more interesting. People can see your illustrations and read your words. *[I remind kids to gather all the supplies they need: markers, pencils, and crayons. After*

TIP: As we compose our summary, I show kids how they can take their information and write it in a more interesting way or merge our thinking with the information.

TIP: We encourage kids to illustrate their new learning because art adds so much to kids' writing.

> **Poisonous Blue Frog Summary**
>
> We learned that there are very, very blue frogs and they are poisonous. The blue frog's bright color is a warning. It says, "stay away from me! I'm poisonous!" We were amazed to learn that when blue frogs eat poisonous ants their skin becomes poisonous! So don't touch those bright blue frogs!

a conversation about how they can illustrate the summary, kids in the small group begin to draw. I move around the room to confer with other students. I notice Joel has a lot of information on Post-its about the jaguar, not all of which is accurate, so I confer with him.]

Read me some of your Post-its, Joel. It looks like you have a lot of information about the jaguar—good for you! You seem to have two questions about what jaguars eat. Let's read them.

Joel: "I wonder if they eat meat. I wonder if they eat leaves."

Where could we find this out? Can you show me where you found the information that made you wonder if jaguars eat leaves? *[Joel pulls out a book and shows me a picture of a jaguar eating an armadillo that is lying on a bed of leaves.]*

Joel: See, the jaguar is eating leaves, right here.

Confer with children to correct misconceptions.

This is so interesting. You inferred from the picture, Joel, that the jaguar is eating leaves. Let's check this out. There is a caption next to the picture. It says that a jaguar is a carnivore, so it has strong teeth. And it says it can eat animals that have tough skins, or even shells like armadillos. So, it sounds like jaguars eat meat; that's what *carnivore* means. Carnivores are animals that eat meat. So what did you learn?

Joel: Whoa! So, it's eating that armadillo, not the leaves.

[Joel writes no! *on his Post-it that says* I wonder if jaguars eat leaves. *He writes his new thought on another Post-it:* The jaguar is eating the armadillo.]

Great thinking, Joel. It's a good idea to confirm what we learn using the picture *and* the words—to make sure our information is accurate. Now we understand that jaguars are meat-eaters because they are carnivores. That means they don't eat plants or leaves and you learned that! Keep reading and I know you will find out some more interesting information.

Share the Learning

[Kids that worked individually and in pairs share a wide range of summaries, from pictures with a few sentences to the small group's summary of the blue poison frog.]

I'm so glad so many of you were willing to share today. Just think about all these different summaries—short ones with a gorgeous picture and a great caption, and long ones that you worked on together. You have done a wonderful job of writing up accurate information and saying what's important, but not telling too much. And you have taught the rest of us so much!

Did your students:

- understand that summarizing information about a topic helps us learn and remember important information?

- use reading, writing, and thinking strategies to create a developmentally appropriate summary?

- merge their thinking with the information to write a summary that is interesting to read and written in authentic voice?

Reflect& Assess

As kids try their hand at summarizing, we first look carefully at the information they have written to make sure it is accurate and in their own words. Language that is taken (almost) straight from the book makes for stilted (and boring) summaries! But many children begin writing summaries that restate the information they want to remember, and that's fine because they have paraphrased it. We encourage kids to incorporate their own background knowledge and ideas into their notes, so that their merged thinking becomes part of the summary. While kids may be asked to write summaries with "just the facts" for state or formal assessment purposes, this is a very specific summary genre. As we assess kids' writing, we look for their authentic voices to shine through and so we guide them to take the information they are learning and shape it into their own thoughts.

Adapt& Differentiate

This lesson was done with first graders, but here are suggestions for how to adapt and differentiate for the whole range of learners.

With kindergarteners, I might read a few sentences about a topic and then ask them to tell me—in just a few words—what they learned. Brevity is the idea here, as we want our summaries to be short and sweet, at least compared to the retellings and recountings children are often asked to do. As we work with little kids, we summarize information orally rather than in writing to get started. And a written summary for a young child might be a phrase or sentence describing their picture.

More experienced readers and writers can organize their Post-its and can take a stab at writing summaries, as the children in the lesson did. Kids need lots of practice with the process, however, so we always begin with oral comments, which we shape and then write into a paragraph. We encourage kids to use Post-its with information so they can actually move the Post-its around on a piece of paper to find the best order for their information. Small-group instruction allows us to make sure every child understands the process and can then work independently. And before kids move to writing, we confer with them to make sure their authentic reactions, responses, and voices haven't gotten lost as they've organized and sequenced their thinking.

First-Grade Summaries

1 This child wrote a short sentence and drew a picture to summarize his learning—a developmentally appropriate summary for him. Sometimes kids start a thought and aren't able to complete it—and then launch into another one. I would review his thinking with him, ask what he would add, and help him expand his thinking and perhaps his writing.

"I know that frogs—that their colors are red, orange, purple, and black dots. They're poisonous."

"I wonder if jaguars eat butterflies."

"A jaguar won't eat a poisonous tree frog."

"I wonder if jaguars chase tree frogs."

"I wonder if jaguars eat meat."

"I learned jaguars attack alligators for their meat."

"They attack alligators when they are sleeping."

2 Joel investigated jaguars and collected his Post-its on paper. He explained: "I had some questions, like 'I wonder if jaguars eat butterflies' and 'I wonder if jaguars chase tree frogs.' But then I thought that jaguars won't eat a poisonous frog, so maybe they don't chase them! Next I wondered if jaguars eat meat. Then I learned that they attack alligators when they are sleeping! Wow! So I learned that jaguars attack alligators for their meat, so I drew the arrows." Joel's explanation provides a window into his line of thinking—how one thought led to another as he researched jaguars. He drew arrows from one Post-it to another during our conversation and he explained how he connected the information, one fact building on another. We encourage children to reason through information and organize it to better understand it. When kids are as eager to research on their own as Joel was, we monitor their progress, intervene when appropriate, but mainly get out of the way and let them have at it.

3 This child learned a lot about jaguars and simply sat down and wrote what she had learned. Rather than a more formal process of transforming notes into sentences, the just "write what you learned" approach makes sense when kids have accurate knowledge and are eager to express and share it.

Name _____ Date _____

Jaggu^ars live in the rainforest. Jaguars sleep in trees. Jaguars are orange with black spots Jaguars are geting KILD because tRees are geting cut Down. they liv in trees

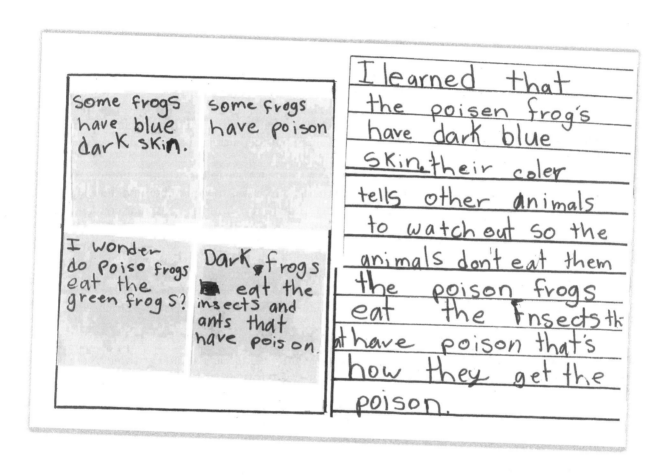

4 This child worked independently to organize her Post-its about the blue poison frog and shaped these notes into a summary. Her summary is a clear recounting of the facts—a good start! I would confer with this child to add punctuation and capital letters where needed. And I would encourage this young author to add some of her own responses or connections to put voice into her writing.

Lesson ⑲ Guide

Use this Lesson Guide and any text of your choice to teach students to create accurate summaries that are full of authentic voice.

Summarize Information

Put it in your own words and keep it interesting

TEACHING MOVES	TEACHING LANGUAGE
	## Connect and Engage
Discuss: What is a *summary* and what is a *topic*?	■ Today we are going to write a *summary*. That means you are going to take only the most important information from your reading or your notes, not every little detail, and write it in your own words. And you want to put some of your own thinking into the summary, too. A *topic* is what we are reading and thinking about. What's our topic today? Right!
Review information kids have learned from reading and taking notes on a topic.	■ Let's review some of what you learned from reading. Turn and talk and then we'll share out the information.
Explain summary writing.	■ When we write a summary, we tell in whole sentences what we have learned that is important to remember about a topic. But first, who wants to share some information that you learned? Great. Go ahead.
Explain note-taking.	■ Notice that I take notes by writing just a few words and paraphrasing the information. Then I'll turn my notes into sentences later on as I write.
	## Model
Explain how to combine information and thinking on a topic to create a group summary.	■ You all mentioned interesting facts about the topic. Now we are going to combine this information into a summary.
	■ Let's go over the information you shared, and I'll write them in sentences to make a paragraph on this Anchor Chart. It will be our summary.
Start with important information and demonstrate how to organize it.	■ I'm going to start with information that tells our readers about our topic. I am thinking about the order in which I will write this information. How about putting…first? Next I will add more of your information and interesting details.
	■ Notice how I incorporated…'s idea…into the summary.
Show how adding questions and thoughts merges thinking with the information.	■ We tell important information, we don't tell too much, and we merge our thinking with the information to make it interesting.
	## Guide
Share an Anchor Chart that lists the steps of writing a summary.	■ Here is a chart to guide us as we write a summary.
	■ You can work on a summary with a small group, or you can continue to take notes on your own or with a partner.

The Teaching Moves outline your instructional sequence and the
Teaching Language gives you an idea about what to say to your students.

TEACHING LANGUAGE	TEACHING MOVES

Collaborate or Practice Independently

- I've pulled this small group together so we can get started writing a summary together. What information do you have?

  Pull a small group together to create a summary with information they have already gathered while the rest of the class works individually or in pairs.

- Let's reread your Post-its and make sure the information is in your own words. Remember that is the first thing on our Anchor Chart about how to write a summary.

  Check to see that the gathered information is in kids' own words and is accurate.

- Let's think about the order in which we want to write our information. Turn and talk about what makes the best first sentence.

- What's next? Here's some interesting information that relates to…. I'll write that in our summary now. Let's reread what we have and see what we want to add next.

  Think about the topic. Then organize and combine the information from Post-its to make sentences.

- It looks like you have a lot of information about…good for you! I notice you have written…. Can you show me where you found information that made you wonder…?

  Respond to kids' individual needs as they read, take notes, and organize information.

- It's a good idea to check what we learn from the picture and the words—to make sure our information is accurate.

  Confer with children to correct misconceptions.

Share the Learning

- Who wants to share a summary with us?

  Have kids share summaries to wrap up the lesson.

- I'm so glad to have seen and heard all these summaries today— short ones with a picture and caption, and long ones that you worked on together.

Reflect & Assess

Did your students:

- understand that summarizing information about a topic helps us learn and remember important information?
- use reading, writing, and thinking strategies to create a developmentally appropriate summary?
- merge their thinking with the information to write a summary that is interesting to read and written in authentic voice?

Read to Get the Big Ideas

Text Matters

As kids build their knowledge about a topic, we seek out books that present ideas in varied and thoughtful ways. Then kids can draw their own conclusions about important issues. As always, we look for well-written text with engaging information. But now, we also open the door to fiction. There are books and stories that are made-up, but that also contain tons of accurate and useful information. Kids can learn from fiction as well as nonfiction, and narratives that combine a story with interesting information add to kids' opportunities to gather valuable ideas about important topics.

Resources & Materials

Lesson Text

The Great Kapok Tree: A Tale of the Amazon Rain Forest by Lynne Cherry (Voyager Books, 1990) [Available in Trade Book Pack.]

Classroom Supplies
- *Character/Big Idea* Anchor Chart
- Marker
- Globe or map of South America

Student Supplies
- Clipboard
- Post-its
- Large blank sheet of paper
- Assorted markers, pencils, and crayons

Synthesize the text

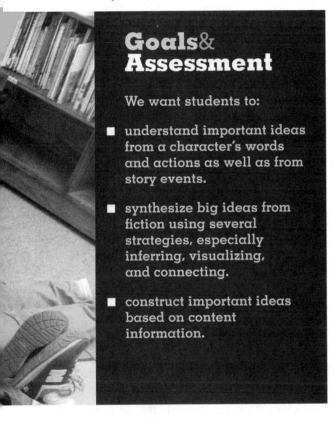

Goals& Assessment

We want students to:

- understand important ideas from a character's words and actions as well as from story events.

- synthesize big ideas from fiction using several strategies, especially inferring, visualizing, and connecting.

- construct important ideas based on content information.

Why & What

As kids build knowledge about a topic, they synthesize the information to understand important ideas and issues. Inferring, visualizing, and questioning are strategies that support synthesizing, and kids use all of these strategies to move beyond factual knowledge about a topic. With fiction, kids often "put themselves in" the story, and this spurs their imaginations about the topic. Narratives, such as *The Great Kapok Tree: A Tale of the Amazon Rain Forest*, add to what kids have already learned from nonfiction so that they construct their own understanding of important ideas. When kids become well informed about a particular subject—grasping big ideas and synthesizing information—they not only learn more, but begin to care more about the topic.

How

Connect and Engage

- Introduce the text and discuss *fiction* as a genre that presents important ideas.

- Activate and connect kids' background knowledge to the topic.

- Begin reading aloud and ask kids to imagine that they are "in" the story.

Model and Guide

- Discuss how to infer meaning from characters' words and actions.

- Explain that authors write books to tell us about important ideas.

- Explain how to use a variety of strategies to understand the story, especially inferring and making connections to background knowledge.

- Show kids how to infer a bigger idea from a character's words and actions.

- Have kids discuss their own versions of the big idea based on their inferences and connections.

- Continue to read aloud and practice inferring big ideas from characters' actions and words, tying thinking to the text.

- Invite kids to discuss their inferences and visual images as they write or draw on Post-its.

- Introduce and explain the idea of *synthesizing*.

- Show kids how to synthesize the big ideas of the whole story.

Collaborate

- Finish the story and invite kids to draw and write their synthesis of the big ideas.

Share the Learning

- Wrap up the lesson by synthesizing the big ideas and suggesting that interested kids do further research.

Lesson Text

The Great Kapok Tree: A Tale of the Amazon Rain Forest is a story in which animals "speak out" and try to persuade a man who is about to cut down their huge, sheltering kapok tree to leave their habitat alone. While very different from the nonfiction or realistic fiction kids have experienced in earlier lessons, this tale of survival in the rain forest is presented in an engaging format that piques kids' curiosity. When teaching kids about the rain forest habitat and its importance to the planet, fiction can present big ideas in a way that kids can grapple with, discuss, and understand.

From *The Great Kapok Tree* by Lynne Cherry. Copyright © 1990. Reprinted by permission of Harcourt, Inc.

TEACHING MOVES   **TEACHING LANGUAGE**

Connect and Engage

Introduce the text and discuss *fiction* as a genre that presents important ideas.

Today we are going to read a book that is very different from the other books about the rain forest we have read. You have learned a lot about the rain forest from nonfiction. We are going to switch gears now and read a story—the author calls it a "tale"—about the rain forest. It is fiction. As you know, *fiction* means the events in the story didn't really happen. But sometimes we learn important ideas from fiction. This book will challenge you to think seriously about the future of the rain forest.

Activate and connect kids' background knowledge to the topic.

TIP: Using a globe or map of South America, locate the Amazon so kids can appreciate its size and length. A globe or map offers a wonderful opportunity to teach geography.

The title of the book is *The Great Kapok Tree: A Tale of the Amazon Rain Forest.* The Amazon River is a huge river flowing through the continent of South America, and there is a lot of rain forest habitat along this river. Here it is on our globe. So it's called the Amazon rain forest. Take a look at the cover of this book. There are some animals you may recognize, living in and around this huge kapok tree. You may already know something about them. Turn and talk. Share what you already know about the animals, this giant tree, and any questions you have. *[After a minute, I ask kids to share out their thinking, especially their background knowledge.]*

Your background knowledge about the rain forest is really growing as we study this topic—and reading this book will add to it. I mentioned that this story is a *tale.* Throughout the story, the animals do the talking, so we know immediately it is fiction. But, as we pay attention to what the animals say, we will learn a lot about an issue that I know is important to you: the survival of the rain forest as a habitat for all kinds of animals. As we meet the animals that are the characters in the story, we will learn some new and perhaps surprising things about them.

TEACHING LANGUAGE

TEACHING MOVES

Let's read the Introduction, which tells us about the book. Close your eyes and imagine you are in the hot, steamy rain forest as I read.

In the Amazon rain forest, it is always hot, and in that heat everything grows and grows and grows. The tops of the trees in the rain forest are called the canopy. The canopy is a sunny place that touches the sky. The animals that live there like lots of light. . . . The bottom of the rain forest is called the understory. The animals that live there like darkness. There, silent snakes curl around hanging vines. Graceful jaguars watch and wait.

Wow, these words really paint a picture in my mind of what it looks and feels like to be in the middle of a rain forest. Are you visualizing and feeling what it's like to sit in the rain forest, with insects buzzing and…

Ella: Howler monkeys howling! That's what they do.

Great idea, Ella. Turn and talk about what you visualize, feel, and maybe even hear. *[Kids turn and talk for a minute. Then I continue reading.]*

And in this steamy environment the great Kapok tree shoots up through the forest and emerges above the canopy. This is the story of a community of animals that live in one such tree in the rain forest.

That's so interesting. The author tells us that this one, big kapok tree—with its huge trunk and vines and leaves that you can see in the picture—is home to a community of animals. That means that all the animals that live in and around this giant tree depend on it for food and a home. Let's look for a minute at how tall the tree is in this picture; you can't even see the top of it! It's full of animals! I see birds soaring around it, a snake slithering down a hanging vine, a monkey swinging through its branches. Keep thinking about the words in the story and the pictures they create in your mind.

Begin reading aloud and ask kids to imagine that they are "in" the story.

TIP: We ask kids to invoke a range of sensory images to fully engage them in the text. Once we have taught kids about visualizing and imagery, we encourage them to continue to imagine a range of sensory images as they listen to or read text.

Model and Guide

Now as I read, I'm going to show you how to infer what's going on in the book—what the animals are doing and saying and what's happening to them. We have inferred and visualized before. Remember how we listen carefully to the author's words and view the pictures to infer and figure out what is going on? Listen now as I read.

Two men walked into the rain forest. Moments before, the forest had been alive with the sounds of squawking birds and howling monkeys. Now all was quiet as the creatures watched the two men and wondered why they had come. The larger man stopped and pointed to a great Kapok tree. Then he left.

The smaller man took the ax he carried and struck the trunk of the tree. Whack! Whack! Whack! . . . Soon the man grew tired. He sat down to rest at the foot of the great Kapok tree. Before he knew it, the heat and hum of the forest had lulled him to sleep.

Discuss how to infer meaning from characters' words and actions.

TIP: We use the model-and-guide approach as the whole lesson is an interactive read-aloud—moving back and forth between showing kids how to think through the story and guiding them to interpret it themselves. During interactive read-alouds, we "catch and release" kids—keeping them up close for a bit and then letting them go to talk and think on their own.

In this story, the author, Lynne Cherry, doesn't tell us why the man is cutting the tree down, but I know from my background knowledge that people cut down trees to use the wood or sell it. And sometimes when the trees are gone, people build houses on the land. Or people might use the land the trees used to be on to plant crops, sometimes for food. I think these might be some of the reasons the two men are trying to cut down the tree. Turn and talk about what you think is happening.

Alyssa: It's too big and thick—that tree. I think he won't be able to cut it down.

Jerome: Why would the man want to cut down such a huge tree, anyway?

Mariah: I infer that would hurt the animals that live there.

Interesting thinking, you all. You used several strategies to think more deeply about what's happening in the story. You inferred what the character was doing, like I did. You asked a question, Jerome, as you tried to understand why this was happening. And, Mariah, you combined your background knowledge with the information in the story to infer that cutting down the tree would be harmful to the animals that live there. It's so important to use your background knowledge and text clues to make inferences when you read.

Let's read the next part.

A boa constrictor lived in the Kapok tree. He slithered down its trunk to where the man was sleeping. He looked at the gash the ax had made in the tree. Then the huge snake slid very close to the man and hissed in his ear "Senhor, this is a tree of miracles. It is my home, where generations of my ancestors have lived. Do not chop it down."

On this page we meet an animal, a boa constrictor, who is telling the sleeping man not to chop down the tree. Watch what I do to respond. I'm going to put what the boa constrictor says into my own words. I think the snake is saying that the tree is amazing—because it gives all the snakes a place to live. And the boa is trying to convince the man not to chop it down. *[I write my thought on the* Character/Big Idea *Anchor Chart so kids can see it.]* Notice the Anchor Chart has a column for the character in the story, in this case, the boa, and another column for the big idea we infer from what the character said and did.

Character

Big Idea
(words/actions)
(what the character said and did)

BOA

The boa said - the tree is amazing and gives all of us snakes a place to live!

Now it's your turn. Turn and talk about the boa constrictor and the big ideas you infer from the story.

[Kids turn and talk for a minute. Then share briefly.]

Zeke: This tree is amazing! All the snake's sisters and brothers live in it—that's the miracle.

You are explaining what the snake said, Zeke. I'm glad you explained the word *miracle* and the idea that all the snake's relatives live in the tree. I'll add that to the *Character/Big Idea* Anchor Chart.

Briana: Wow. The snake's ancestors lived there—that's how old it is! So the snake says, "Please don't cut it down!"

Zachary: When trees are cut down, they are gone! I have a connection. I read a book about that!

I'll add Briana's thought to the chart—about how old the tree is. That's important. Good point, Zachary. You made a connection to a book you read that gave you some important information. Once trees are cut down, it takes a long time for them to grow back. And if people build houses on the land or plant crops, the trees don't grow back at all. Part of the rain forest is gone forever! I'll add what you both said to the Anchor Chart. *[I add students' inferences to the* Character/Big Idea *Anchor Chart.]*

You each had your own thoughts, and you inferred and made connections to the big ideas. That's what good readers do to understand what they read. They make inferences about what the characters said and did as they think for themselves to come up with big ideas that are not exactly written in the story. Or they make connections to what they know or have learned about rain forests to better understand the story.

Have kids discuss their own versions of the big idea based on their inferences and connections.

TIP: In this lesson, we move away from teacher modeling to more of a guided discussion that incorporates kids' comments. As soon as kids are ready, they become part of the discussion as we all think through the text together.

TIP: We use language that labels the strategies kids are using to understand, such as making inferences and connections. As we teach explicitly, we constantly reiterate strategy language, such as "I infer" or "I have a connection" to support kids to articulate their thinking.

Character

Big Idea

(words/actions)
(what the character said and did)

BOA

The boa said - the tree is amazing and gives all of us snakes a place to live!

All my brothers and sisters live in this amazing tree - that's the miracle (Zeke)

The tree is old - so the snake says "Please don't cut it down!" (Briana)

When trees get cut down, they are gone! (Zachary)

Continue to read aloud and practice inferring big ideas from characters' actions and words, tying thinking to the text.

Now it is your turn to practice inferring the big idea. Sometimes we'll turn and talk, or you can do this on your own. Go ahead and write your thinking about the big ideas on a Post-it.

I am going to continue reading. Listen to what the next character says.

A bright and small tree frog crawled along the edge of a leaf. In a squeaky voice he piped in the man's ear: "Senhor, a ruined rain forest means ruined lives...many ruined lives. You will leave many of us homeless if you chop down this great Kapok tree."

Turn and talk. What do you think about the tree frog's message? *[After a moment or two, we come back together.]*

Jared: The animals won't have a place to live without the tree. If animals don't have a place to live, maybe they will die.

Good inference, Jared. You inferred that the word *homeless* meant the animals wouldn't have anywhere to live if the tree is cut down. Take a minute to think about the big idea here. You can write and/or draw your understanding.

[I keep reading the story, and kids are still up close with clipboards and Post-its so that they can continue responding during this interactive read-aloud. I stop every few pages and ask kids to turn and talk about the animals in the story and then write or draw their responses.]

Invite kids to discuss their inferences and visual images as they write or draw on Post-its.

Introduce and explain the idea of *synthesizing*.

Now we are going to do something really important as we read the end of the story. We have been focusing on the characters' words and actions to understand some big ideas. Now we're going to think about all of the characters and all of the events in the story to figure out what the author most wants us to learn and remember about the topic. This is called *synthesizing*, a pretty big word for sure. When we synthesize, we put all of our thinking together—our connections, our questions, and our inferences—to make sense of the whole story.

[I read aloud a few more pages, pausing after the boy's words.]

"Senhor, when you awake, please look upon us all with new eyes."

Show kids how to synthesize the big ideas of the whole story.

I infer from the boy's words—"please look upon us all with new eyes"—that he is asking the man to see the animals in a new way. No longer will the man want to cut down the kapok tree. Instead he will see the wonderful animals that live there and how important that tree is to their survival. I am *synthesizing* what the characters—the animals—have been saying and doing to make sense of the whole story. That's what I am thinking. Now I'm curious to know what you are thinking.

Joel: I think he hears the animals and the boy in his dreams.

Anna: I infer he will change his mind and not cut down the tree. He might feel bad for the animals.

Rachel: Maybe he is just going to go away when he wakes up.

Ezekiel: The animals spoke to the man when he was sleeping. He woke up and saw how amazing the animals of the rain forest are!

Such great thinking, you are really beginning to understand the important ideas in the story! I can visualize what's happening at the end of the story from your words. And now you'll have a chance to draw the big ideas. When we use all of our strategies to make sense of the story, we are synthesizing. Let's read the last page to make sure we are getting the big idea here.

Collaborate

[I read the end of the story. In the end, the man who was going to cut down the tree abandons his ax and departs.]

Now I'd like you to look over your Post-its to try to synthesize what you think are the most important ideas in the story. Take the Post-its you've written and put them on your own piece of poster paper. You can illustrate some of the big ideas you've written on your Post-its. When you put all your thinking together, try to come up with the big ideas for the whole story. I can hardly wait to hear and see what you draw and write.

[Kids go off and work collaboratively. I confer with them along the way. Then we come back together.]

Finish the story and invite kids to draw and write their synthesis of the big ideas.

Share the Learning

Who would like to share what they wrote and drew?

Ansel: So he put down the ax and walked away! He didn't cut the tree down after all!

Briana: I think the man started to care about the animals.

Jacob: The writer wants us to not cut down the trees in the rain forest.

You have such great thoughts and such amazing illustrations! Both your words and pictures show the important ideas in this story. You put together what the characters said and did with the events of the story to really understand the big ideas.

From your writing and drawing I can tell that you understand and share the author's concern that the rain forests are disappearing and being cut down all over the world. I can tell you are synthesizing some big ideas. Rain forests are endangered, and the author wants to help save them because they are so important for a healthy Earth! Ella suggested that we write letters to people who are cutting down the forests and share our ideas about why rain forests should be protected. If there is anyone who would like to do some research on why the rain forests are being cut down and what we can do about it, please talk with Ella. When you know a lot about something, you begin to care more about it. And when we care about something, like the rain forest, sometimes we can take action to protect and save it.

Wrap up the lesson by synthesizing the big ideas and suggesting that interested kids do further research.

Did your students:

- understand important ideas from a character's words and actions as well as from story events?

- synthesize big ideas from fiction using several strategies, especially inferring, visualizing, and connecting?

- construct important ideas based on content information?

Reflect & Assess

As kids build their background knowledge about the rain forest, we encourage them to move from a focus on facts and information to consideration of big ideas and issues. The tale of *The Great Kapok Tree* provides an opportunity for kids to figure out and synthesize big ideas related to the rain forest. We examine kids' responses to see how they use strategies such as connecting and inferring to put the big ideas in their own words. As kids collect their Post-its at the end of the story, synthesizing the most important ideas for the whole story helps them to share their insights about a topic they have come to care deeply about.

Adapt & Differentiate

This lesson was done with first graders, but here are suggestions for how to adapt and differentiate with the whole range of learners.

With younger readers, such as kindergarteners and these first graders, the whole lesson works best as an interactive read-aloud. For the youngest children, I would read the story over several sittings, and paraphrase the actions and words of the animals in the story in simpler language. We would work together at the end of the story to draw and scribe the kids' ideas of what the story was all about—drawing and writing all of our thinking on a big piece of chart paper.

With older, more experienced readers, I would stop frequently and let them infer and visualize the characters' actions and words in words and pictures. Rather than thinking through the last pages of the story together, I'd read the end aloud and let the kids figure out and synthesize the big ideas of the story. They could work out their thinking on their own or with a partner, and then we could come back together to share their different ideas and interpretations.

First-Grade Responses

1 After we finished reading the story, this child drew the man with his ax on his shoulder, saying "I think he stopped because he remembered what the animals said." His comment was scribed; he spent most of the time illustrating his synthesis of the story which his picture clearly communicates.

2 This student responded with two Post-its as she listened to the read aloud. An English Language Learner, she asked for help writing her thoughts. She asked, "I wonder if the man can hear the animals talking to him? I infer that he can!" and then answered her own question. She was able to infer from the character's words and actions. She also added information about the jaguar's message: "A jaguar came to tell the man that he could not cut down his tree. That's how the jaguar gets his food." After going off to finish her poster at the end of the lesson, she returned with additional illustrations and her synthesis: "The man started to care about the animals." With ongoing discussion and plenty of time to process a story such as this one, kids begin to construct the important ideas in texts for themselves.

The jaguar said to the man, Senhor I live in the Kapok tree. If you cut it down I won't have food or shelter)

The Great Kapok Tree

The anteater istelling the man whle he cuts Down the tree the BaBBy anumuls Well Be Borne in a World Wethout tree.

3 These children illustrated and para-phrased the animals in the story, but they did not take their thinking to the point of synthesizing a big idea. We celebrate that they understood and can articulate these, but I would confer with them to nudge them toward a bigger idea. Learning to synthesize is a process that kids need to practice, so we provide many opportunities to do this.

"The anteater is telling the man when he cuts down the tree the baby animals will be born in a world without trees."

Read to Get the Big Ideas

Synthesize the text

TEACHING MOVES	TEACHING LANGUAGE
	Connect and Engage
Introduce the text and discuss *fiction* as a genre that presents important ideas.	■ We are going to read a story about…. It is *fiction*, which means the events in the story didn't happen, but there could be lots of useful and accurate information in there.
Activate and connect kids' background knowledge to the topic.	■ Take a look at this cover. There are some…you may recognize…. You may already know something about…. Turn and talk about what you are thinking and any questions you have.
Begin reading aloud and ask kids to imagine that they are "in" the story.	■ As I read, close your eyes and imagine you are in the story. Are you visualizing and feeling what it's like to be…? Turn and talk about what you visualize, feel, and maybe even hear.
	Model and Guide
Discuss how to infer meaning from characters' words and actions.	■ Now as I read, I'm going to infer what's going on. Remember how we listened to the author's words and looked at the pictures to figure out what was going on?
Explain that authors write books to tell us about important ideas.	■ In this story, the author tells us about…. And I know from my background knowledge that…. I think these might be some of the reasons why….
	■ Turn and talk. What do you think are some of the author's big ideas in the story so far?
Explain how to use a variety of strategies to understand the story, especially inferring and making connections to background knowledge.	■ You used several strategies to think more deeply about what's happening in the story. It's so important to use all your reading strategies to understand what you read.
Show kids how to infer a bigger idea from a character's words and actions.	■ After I read this part, I'm going to put what the character says into my own words. I ask myself…. I think…. Let me write that on the Anchor Chart.
Have kids discuss their own versions of the big idea based on their inferences and connections.	■ How would you put what the character is saying and doing into your own words? That's an interesting thought. I'll add that to the Anchor Chart.
Continue to read aloud and practice inferring big ideas from characters' actions and words, tying thinking to the text.	■ I'm going to continue reading. What do you think about…? Remember to tie your thinking to the text. Everyone write and draw what you think…. I'll add your thoughts to the Anchor Chart.

The Teaching Moves outline your instructional sequence and the Teaching Language gives you an idea about what to say to your students.

TEACHING LANGUAGE	TEACHING MOVES
■ I will keep reading the story. Every few pages I'll stop so you can turn and talk about…. Then draw or write what you are inferring and visualizing.	Invite kids to discuss their inferences and visual images as they write or draw on Post-its.
■ Now that we are coming to the end of the story, we are going to synthesize…in order to understand the big ideas the author wrote about. *Synthesize* means to put things together.	Introduce and explain the idea of *synthesizing*.
■ Let me read the last few pages to you. I infer from…. I'm thinking that…. I am synthesizing to make sense of the whole story. When we think about the story and the big ideas, we are synthesizing.	Show kids how to synthesize the big ideas of the whole story.

Collaborate

■ I'd like you to synthesize what you think are the most important ideas in the story. Draw or write your thinking on this big paper and add your Post-its. I can hardly wait to see what you draw and write.	Finish the story and invite kids to draw and write their synthesis of the big ideas.

Share the Learning

■ From your writing and drawing, I can see you're synthesizing the big ideas. We can also investigate further if we have some questions we want to find out more about. Or you can also take action by letting people know your ideas and opinions!	Wrap up the lesson by synthesizing the big ideas and suggesting that interested kids do further research.

Reflect & Assess

Did your students:

■ understand important ideas from a character's words and actions as well as from story events?

■ synthesize big ideas from fiction using several strategies, especially inferring, visualizing, and connecting?

■ construct important ideas based on content information?

Explore and Investigate

Text Matters

When we embark on extended, ambitious research units with kids, we want to be sure the classroom has an abundance of materials on the topic kids are investigating. We check to see if we have a variety of formats, text with clear and accurate information, and kid-friendly layouts that include JEI (just enough information), as opposed to TMI (too much information). We make sure the photographs and illustrations are compelling and complement the text. We choose books with a table of contents and index so that kids can easily find information they are looking for. Visual and text features (such as maps, diagrams, charts, and close-ups) present information that kids can access without slogging through long paragraphs of dense text. And with informative books like *The Great Kapok Tree* in mind, we include relevant fiction selections as well.

Resources & Materials

Lesson Text

TIME For Kids Bigger Picture Edition [Spring 2003] "Welcome to the Rain Forest" poster

The Great Kapok Tree: A Tale of the Amazon Rain Forest by Lynne Cherry (Voyager Books, 1990) [Available in Trade Book Pack.]

Additional Text

Abundant text on the topic of study with a variety of formats, clear and accurate information, and kid-friendly layout

Classroom Supplies

- *Steps for Researching* Anchor Chart
- Chart paper and marker

Student Supplies

- Poster paper, markers, scissors, and glue sticks
- Post-its

Read, write, and draw in a researcher's workshop

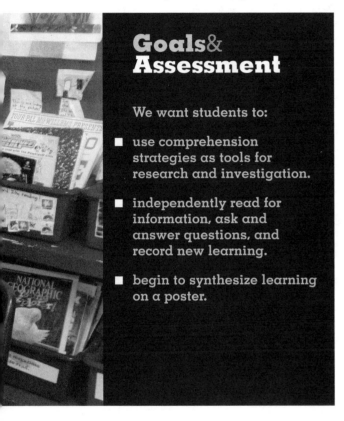

Goals& Assessment

We want students to:

- use comprehension strategies as tools for research and investigation.

- independently read for information, ask and answer questions, and record new learning.

- begin to synthesize learning on a poster.

Why&What

Comprehension strategies are tools kids use over and over again as they do research as part of a classroom unit of study. Our definition of research is broad: notice and pursue new learning, ask and answer questions, summarize information, and put all new learning together through drawing and writing. The classroom is transformed into a researcher's workshop, where kids read, write, talk, draw, and investigate over several days. We first review strategies for learning from nonfiction. When kids are ready to synthesize their learning, we show them how to create a poster—where they collect their Post-its and notes as well as illustrate and write what they have learned. Most of the teaching takes place during conferences so we can respond to kids' individual learning needs and interests while they research and create posters during researcher's workshop.

How

Connect and Engage

- Co-construct an Anchor Chart that guides kids as they do research.

Model

- Model how to put Post-its with information and questions on a poster. Draw and label the picture.

- Use a child's example to show how to begin research and find an answer to a question.

- Support the child to articulate what he or she did and link it to what researchers do. Paraphrase and reiterate the process to be sure that kids understand it.

Guide

- Ask kids to share their plans for research during independent work time.

Collaborate or Practice Independently

- Continue to teach through conferences to differentiate instruction during researcher's workshop. Remind kids to consult the Anchor Chart for guidance.

- Confer with kids to focus them on specific research questions and make sure they are on the right track.

Share the Learning

- Select kids to share work that demonstrates how to put all their thinking together on a poster.

- Point out how a child synthesized and organized learning.

- Let kids know that an Anchor Chart with suggestions for creating a poster will include their ideas.

Lesson Text

To build on what kids learned from the *TFK* "Welcome to the Rain Forest" poster and *The Great Kapok Tree*, we now add materials with different formats so that the writing serves as a model for kids' summaries, posters, and projects. Books with a question/answer format are great for kids who are reading to answer questions. They learn that answers are often brief and to the point. Materials, books, and online sources with features (such as maps, charts, and glossaries) spark kids to use features in their own posters and written work. As kids engage in research, we encourage them to take on at least one informational text as a "mentor text" and use its patterns and structures to help them create their own writing.

From *The Great Kapok Tree* by Lynne Cherry. Copyright © 1990. Reprinted by permission of Harcourt, Inc.

Used with permission from *Time For Kids*.

TEACHING MOVES	TEACHING LANGUAGE

Connect and Engage

Co-construct an Anchor Chart that guides kids as they do research.

Does anyone know what a researcher is? Turn and talk about what you think a researcher does. *[Kids share out the following which I jot down on an Anchor Chart:]*

"Read a book and write down what I learned and what I wonder."

"A researcher asks and answers questions."

TIP: We often ask kids to share what's on their minds about a question we ask them. We list their thoughts on Anchor Charts, but we don't forget to weigh in ourselves to add to and clarify their thinking, or add something that has not been mentioned that we think is important. If kids are getting antsy with all this writing, we take a break or continue to create the chart the next day.

> Researchers...
>
> Read, notice, and record new learning
>
> Wonder about information and investigate it
>
> Ask and answer questions
>
> Observe carefully and draw what they are learning
>
> Write up their learning
>
> Use lots of features to show learning:
> Captions and pictures
> Labels and pictures
> Maps
> Close-ups
> Cutaways
> Diagrams
>
> Synthesize new information to share it and teach it to others

"I watched a salamander and drew it sleeping!"

"Write the facts. Also, in my research, I drew pictures, cutaways, and close-ups. I added captions to my picture, too."

Wow! Researchers do all these things and as you can see, I've written them on an Anchor Chart. As we have been reading and learning from nonfiction, you all have become researchers. You know how to find answers to your questions, which you pointed out is something that researchers do all the time. You keep track of your thinking—on Post-its and in your notes. And you are careful observers so you can draw your learning, too.

But we can't forget one more thing! Researchers love to teach people what they have learned. They synthesize all their new learning so they can teach that information to others. I'll add this to the chart.

Model

Today you are going to keep doing research, learning new information, asking and answering questions, and writing and drawing what you learn. We'll be doing this in researcher's workshop. That's just like reader's workshop, when we read and respond to our reading. It's also like writer's workshop, when we write and draw and then we talk about and share our writing with each other. We do research—reading, writing, drawing, talking, and listening as we investigate our class topic—the rain forest. You all know a lot about the rain forest already, and I am going to show you how I organize and synthesize what I have learned on a poster.

Model how to put Post-its with information and questions on a poster. Draw and label the picture.

I'm going to model for you how I make a poster about the horned katydid. *[I begin to draw and add Post-its, saying what I do, as I do it.]* I draw my picture and label it. It's just fine to put Post-its with information on your poster, so I'm going to do that. I put up my Post-its that show what I learned on this big piece of paper. I learned that the katydid has horns and spikes. I learned that if insects try to eat it, they get a mouthful of spikes. Then I add my Post-its with questions. I'm still researching these. And I just answered one of my questions about what they eat, so I wrote the answer on the Post-it with the question. And that's my katydid poster!

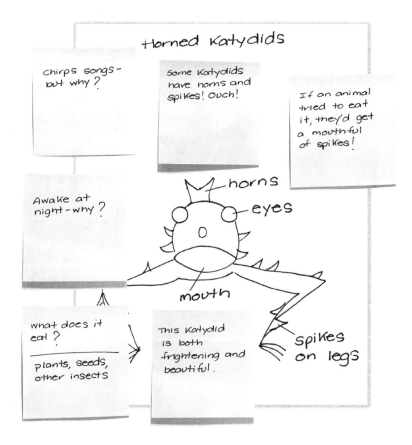

Natalia has offered to share what she's been doing to research a topic she wondered about—night monkeys. She is going to show you how she wondered about night monkeys and how she did her research. Tell us how you got interested in night monkeys, Natalia.

Natalia: I was doing rain forest research. I learned that the night monkey is the only nocturnal monkey. I wrote that in my notebook and wondered, "Can I study night monkeys?"

Will you share what you wrote in your notebook?

Natalia: I wrote "The night monkey is the only nocturnal monkey on the whole earth. There are so many kinds of monkeys in the world, but the night monkey is the only nocturnal monkey in the world!"

This will help all of us to think about our research, because now we know how you started yours. You were curious about an animal because it is so unusual. It is the only monkey in the whole world that is awake and active at night—that's what *nocturnal* means. Will you share one of your questions? And I think you found an answer to your question—so share that with us, too.

Natalia: My question was, "What do night monkeys eat?"

TIP: When we ask kids to share how they do research, we guide them as they describe what they were thinking and what they did. When kids take their thinking public in this way, all our kids listen and learn what to do.

Notice that Natalia wrote her question at the top of the page. Would you read it—and your answer, too?

Natalia: "What do night monkeys eat? They feed on fruit, leaves, insects, and other small animals. Night monkeys use their big eyes to see in the dark. They use their big eyes to catch food."

Can you tell us more about how you found the answer to your question?

Natalia: I found a book about monkeys. I looked in the table of contents of the book and saw "Nocturnal Monkeys, pages 28 and 29." I knew night monkeys are nocturnal so I turned to the pages and saw the night monkey and found what they eat. I saw a picture of the jungle gold beetle. That's an insect it eats, so I drew it. I learned they eat fruit, leaves, insects, and other little animals, and I wrote that down.

Natalia, you are quite a researcher! Notice that she read with her question in mind; she used the table of contents and found the pages for the topic she was interested in. Then she read the pages and found information that answered her question about what night monkeys eat. She thought about the information, wrote some of it down, and drew a picture. You can put all this up on your poster, if you like, Natalia! Now, everyone, it's your turn.

Support the child to articulate what he or she did and link it to what researchers do. Paraphrase and reiterate the process to be sure that kids understand it.

TIP: This child is putting into practice several strategies taught previously: how to read with a question in mind and use text features, such as a table of contents, to find information. Using children's work and examples as much as possible to review skills and strategies empowers kids as both teachers and learners.

Guide

Ask kids to share their plans for research during independent work time.

TIP: We ask kids to share out what they plan to do during the workshop so they have a clear focus for independent work time. We also make sure all the materials kids need are easily accessible so that they spend their time on research rather than on retrieving materials!

Let's review our chart of what researchers do. It will guide you as you work on your own. Before we go off, I'd like to hear about what some of you plan to do during researcher's workshop. Who would like to begin? *[Kids share out what they will do next.]*

Ansel: I'm going to go on the computer and find out what harpy eagles eat.

Belinda: I heard there were poisonous butterflies, so I want to know which ones are poisonous. I'll read my book about butterflies.

Jared: I'm going to put my Post-its about the emerald tree boa on my poster and make a **big** picture of it!

These are great questions and ideas for doing research. If you would like paper to make a poster, I will leave it right here and you can get it yourself. Happy researching!

Collaborate or Practice Independently

Continue to teach through conferences to differentiate instruction during researcher's workshop. Remind kids to consult the Anchor Chart for guidance.

Confer with kids to focus them on specific research questions and make sure they are on the right track.

TIP: In this researcher's workshop, we model and guide a bit as kids conduct their research, but most instruction takes place during conferences, because at this point the teaching is individualized. Kids are at many different points in the research process. Some need help reading sources, others need support to organize the information they're gathering, and still others want to get my response to their writing or drawings. When kids are really engaged in their research, they clamor for opportunities to have at it.

I'll come around to confer with you about what you are doing. If you get stuck and aren't sure what to do next, come take a look at our Anchor Chart!

[I confer with Nolan who is interested in crocodiles.] What are the questions you are interested in researching?

Nolan: I know what crocodiles and alligators eat. But I wonder what animal eats crocodiles.

I see you have some books on these animals. What would you do to find information to answer this question?

Nolan: I think anacondas might eat crocodiles, so I could check what anacondas eat.

[He looks up anaconda *in the index of his book and turns to the listed pages.]*

Nolan: Here's a picture. It's a snake wrapped around a crocodile. It's a boa! That's it! A boa is also an anaconda.

Be sure, Nolan, to read the caption that goes with that photograph, OK? We want to make sure we understand what's happening in the photo and that your information is accurate. *[I continue conferring with Nolan to find and record an answer and ask him to share his research process with the class.]*

Share the Learning

You did a great job working on all your research today. Now we are going to review how you can organize your thinking and information on a poster. Remember, a poster is a place to put your Post-its and notes and add your thinking and learning as you go. You'll also want to illustrate your information with pictures and use features so that you can teach what you have learned to others.

Nolan spent a lot of time organizing his learning about crocodiles on a poster. He's agreed to share how he put all his thinking together on his poster. There are many ways to make a poster, but Nolan is going to show us one way. Nolan, tell us what you did.

> Nolan: I drew a big picture of a crocodile and wrote "crocodiles" in big letters. That's the title of my poster. I labeled all the parts of the crocodile in my picture. Then I learned that boas—they are anacondas—eat crocodiles so I drew the boa squeezing the crocodile. Then I learned that birds and snakes eat crocodile eggs.

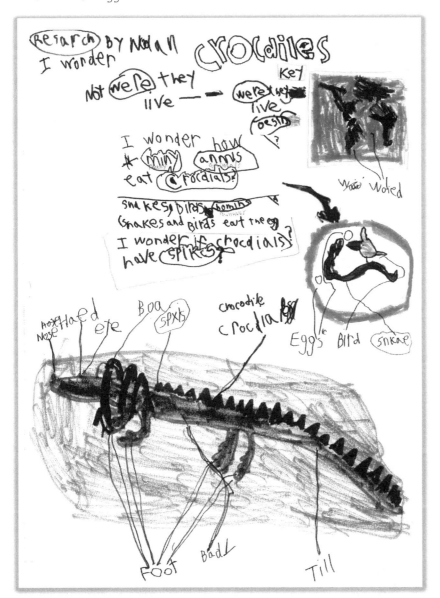

Select kids to share work that demonstrates how to put all their thinking together on a poster.

TIP: There are many ways to begin a poster—so it makes sense to ask several kids to share so that children see various entry points. Also, if you offer just one model, kids are more likely to think it is the "right" one and try to imitate it.

TIP: We seldom hear the words, "I'm done," echoing around the classroom during researcher's workshop. When kids finish a poster or other project, they are eager to keep investigating and learning because they are free to choose a book to read or an interest to pursue. Choice and ownership foster engagement.

Let's see, Nolan. It looks like the information that birds and snakes eat crocodile eggs answers one of your questions.

Nolan: Yeah, that answered my question about how many animals eat crocodiles—if they eat the eggs, they are eating baby crocodiles. I drew an arrow from my question to that information. Then I saw a map, so I drew that on my poster. It shows where crocodiles live and not where they live, so I made a map. I made a key with the colors.

Point out how a child synthesized and organized learning.

Wow, Nolan. That's a great explanation of how you created your poster. We can all see how you connected your question to the information that answered it and how you organized your learning. Features like the map really give us a lot of information about where crocodiles live. Nolan, would you like to ask if anyone has any questions or comments?

Nolan: Any questions or comments?

Bryan: How did you start?

Nolan: I drew the picture of the crocodile first and I put on the labels to show its parts. Then I wrote the title. I had the questions on Post-its so I put them on it. Then I found some information that answered my questions and drew it.

So you see you can start with Post-its you've done, or a big illustration. And you can keep adding new learning to your poster as you find out more! So great!

[After the lesson I create a chart to guide kids as they begin to gather their thinking and learning and organize it onto a poster. As I talk and work with kids, I am careful to emphasize that there are many entry points for beginning to create a poster:]

Let kids know that an Anchor Chart with suggestions for creating a poster will include their ideas.

TIP: Sometimes it makes sense to create Anchor Charts over time rather than all at once. With beginning researchers, we would begin with only two or three suggestions for creating a poster, adding more as we modeled what to do over several days. When we do research, it's all about teaching the researchers, not completing a project—so we adapt our pace to our kids' needs.

Creating a Poster

- Draw, draw, draw. Create illustrations to show your learning.

- Add captions or labels to tell about the pictures.

- Collect your Post-its and put them on a poster.

- or write your new learning and questions right on the poster.

- organize your new learning so that a reader can understand it.

- Readers want to learn from your poster so make your writing and drawing BIG and VISIBLE.

- Use features to show your information. And don't forget to put a title on your poster!

Did your students:

- use comprehension strategies as tools for research and investigation?

- independently read for information, ask and answer questions, and record new learning?

- begin to synthesize learning on a poster?

Reflect & Assess

Children's innate curiosity and fascination with the real world spur them to use the reading and thinking strategies in the service of research and investigation. To assess how well kids have mastered reading for information, asking and answering questions, and summarizing their learning, we look carefully at their work and confer with them daily.

As they complete their research posters, we see right before our eyes what skills kids have in reading, researching, writing, organizing, illustrating, and sharing complex information. We study those artifacts, display them, and save them as evidence of kids' thinking in action.

Adapt & Differentiate

In any given classroom, kids are at very different points in their reading and writing development, so researcher's workshop lets us differentiate and individualize instruction. With very young children, we would begin research in small groups, each group investigating one aspect of a topic under study. We commandeer every available adult to guide these small groups, knowing that kids need support to ask a question and then try to find the answer to it. We also model asking and answering questions in a large group—writing a question and then drawing answers to it as we discover new information. Much of this beginning work is done orally or with kids drawing pictures that show their learning. Posters can be simple or sophisticated. What matters is that kids are summarizing and demonstrating their thinking and learning.

As kids become more practiced with asking researchable questions and organizing information, we continue with lessons that remind kids how they can use comprehension strategies as tools. The goal as kids get older is to use strategies flexibly—applying them as needed as they read, write, and think across the curriculum. Short sharing sessions allow kids to teach their peers about their own original ideas for gathering and organizing information. As they share their creative approaches to sharing their information, the whole group learns new and original ways of taking their thinking public.

1 Natalia put her notebook page, a glossary, her question about night monkeys and what they eat, and her notes organized into columns (I Wonder/I Learned/Wow!) on her poster, which she completed over several weeks' time. Her illustrations tied together the information and provided the finishing touches to this amazing synthesis of her learning. Natalia demonstrated her clear understanding of reading, writing, drawing, and thinking as tools for learning and wrote up what she did to research night monkeys (see her page of writing below).

Kindergarten Posters

2 Our youngest students create posters in small groups. As this class studied African animals, children drew and painted what they had learned, writing information on sentence strips and adding these to the poster. Little kids love working big and we launch them into research early and often! The piece of paper at the bottom of this poster says, "Please write your questions, comments, and connections here." This invites students who are reading and learning from the poster to write a response.

First-Grade Mobile (3) and Poster (4)

3 This child's interest in galaxies led to a "poster-cum-mobile" entitled "Irregular Galaxy." One reason why kids love creating posters and "working big" is that they can put their imagination and original ideas to work to show their learning in a myriad of ways.

4 These children collaborated on a poster about birds of prey. The poster reveals both information and responses that include these ideas among others:

"The eagle's talons are like vice grips."

"Eagles ride on air currents."

"I think if the fish die out, the birds of prey will be scarce. The birds will not have fish to eat."

They also include new information and one child makes a connection to his mother, saying, "I know my mom used to help birds. [Here's] my mom with an eagle. (Arrow to drawing.) She's wearing a special glove."

Kids represent their thinking and learning in all sorts of ways, incorporating knowledge gained from reading and personal experience.

This Lesson Guide can help you teach students to explore a topic using multiple strategies and create a research poster that summarizes their learning.

Explore and Investigate

Read, write, and draw in a researcher's workshop

TEACHING MOVES	TEACHING LANGUAGE
	Connect and Engage
Co-construct an Anchor Chart that guides kids as they do research.	▪ Many of you are interested in learning more about…. Let's start by listing how we find out more information or answer a question.
	Model
Model how to put Post-its with information and questions on a poster. Draw and label the picture.	▪ I'm going to model for you how I make a poster about my topic…. I'll put Post-its with information and my questions on it. I'll draw a picture and label it. I can continue to add to my poster if I find more information.
Use a child's example to show how to begin research and find an answer to a question.	▪ …is going to show you how she wondered about her topic and then did her research.
	▪ You were curious; you had a question. Then you found an answer. Tell us how you found that information.
Support the child to articulate what he or she did and link it to what researchers do. Paraphrase and reiterate the process to be sure that kids understand it.	▪ You used text features and visual features. You thought about the information, wrote it down, and drew a picture. You can put all of this on your poster. Thanks for sharing how you began to put your information together. You have taught all of us how to do research!
	Guide
Ask kids to share their plans for research during independent work time.	▪ Let's review our chart of what researchers do.
	▪ Who'd like to tell us what they plan to be researching during our workshop time today? Wonderful,…. Who else? If you'd like paper to make a poster, it's right here. Some of you may be reading, learning, and asking questions. Some of you may be putting all your information on a poster. Researchers do all of those things!

The Teaching Moves outline your instructional sequence and the
Teaching Language gives you an idea about what to say to your students.

TEACHING LANGUAGE	TEACHING MOVES

Collaborate or Practice Independently

- You are welcome to work on your own, with a partner, or in a small group. I'll come around to confer with you about what you are doing. You can look at the chart we created about what researchers do for guidance.

Continue to teach through conferences to differentiate instruction during researcher's workshop. Remind kids to consult the Anchor Chart for guidance.

- What is it you are interested in researching?
- I see you have some material here about…. What would you do to find information to answer this question? How could we be sure that this is accurate information…? I'll check back with you in a while to see how you are doing with your questions.

Confer with kids to focus them on specific research questions and make sure they are on the right track.

Share the Learning

- Who would like to share their research with the class?
- …has offered to talk to us about researching…. …will share how you can wonder, ask questions, and pursue answers and how you organize and put together all your thinking on a poster.

Select kids to share work that demonstrates how to put all their thinking together on a poster.

- Wow,…, we can all see your new learning and how you organized your thinking!

Point out how a child synthesized and organized learning.

- Now we're going to review how you can organize your thinking on a poster. I'll be creating an Anchor Chart that captures your thinking about this process and can guide you as you make your own posters.

Let kids know that an Anchor Chart with suggestions for creating a poster will include their ideas.

Reflect & Assess

Did your students:

- use comprehension strategies as tools for research and investigation?
- independently read for information, ask and answer questions, and record new learning?
- begin to synthesize learning on a poster?

Share Your Learning

Text Matters

In this lesson, kids continue to use a variety of published materials on the classroom topic study. The research posters, poems, and books kids create also serve as texts for classmates to read. Student projects become examples that jump-start their peers' efforts to organize, synthesize, and share information. Great student-created examples allow kids to visualize how their learning might take shape. We keep copies of previous projects, posters, books, and poems so that this year's kids can learn from the thoughtful, creative kids who have come before them.

Resources & Materials

Lesson Text

Samples of kids' successful projects, posters, poems, and books

Text on the classroom topic of study with variety of formats, with clear and accurate information and kid-friendly layouts

Rain Forest Poetry Word Chart

Classroom Supplies
- Chart paper and marker
- Books on the rain forest and related topics
- Teacher-created book on the study topic

Student Supplies
- Poster paper, markers, scissors, and glue sticks
- Blank booklets
- Post-its

Create projects to demonstrate understanding

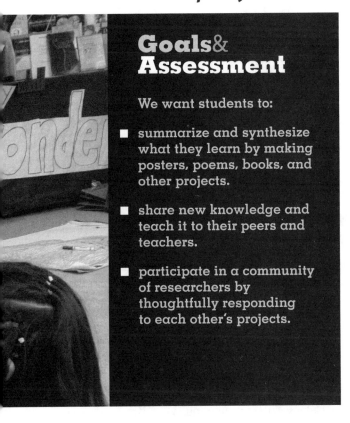

Goals& Assessment

We want students to:

- summarize and synthesize what they learn by making posters, poems, books, and other projects.

- share new knowledge and teach it to their peers and teachers.

- participate in a community of researchers by thoughtfully responding to each other's projects.

How [Watch this lesson on the *PTK* DVD-ROM.]

Connect and Engage

- Review how to make a poster and introduce other ways to share learning—making a poem or a book.

- Review making a poster using a child's example or using the poster modeled in Lesson 21.

Model and Guide

- Model writing poetry as one way to synthesize and share new learning.

- Model and share words that describe visual images and sounds.

- Model how to write and illustrate a book, another way to synthesize and share new knowledge.

Collaborate or Practice Independently

- Give kids options for doing research: reading, writing, and thinking about information or working on a project to synthesize their learning.

Share the Learning

- Ask kids to share their poems, posters, and books.

- Teach kids ways to respond to and discuss their peers' projects.

- Invite kids to respond through writing and drawing and adding comments to their classmates' work.

Why & What

Teaching others what they have learned provides kids with an authentic purpose for "putting it all together," or synthesizing their learning. Once kids summarize and synthesize their information, they enthusiastically share this new knowledge with peers and teachers alike. Researcher's workshop provides kids with time to draw and write posters, poems, books, and other projects. When kids realize they can choose how to synthesize and share their learning, the sky's the limit! In this lesson, we review how to make a poster and model how to write nonfiction poems and books. We also teach kids ways to respond to each other's work during sharing time. Kids respond orally and in writing, offering comments, asking questions, and building on each other's thinking. In this way, the classroom becomes a community where everyone is both a teacher and a learner.

Lesson Text

Kids create original projects to summarize and synthesize thinking when we provide them with examples—from published nonfiction texts and from the work their peers have done. Many times, kids get their best ideas from each other. Lesson texts here include kids' work, such as Briana's poster on jaguars (see next page) or Ezekiel's poster about snakes (see page 56). We share word charts of poetic language to support kids to write poetry about the rain forest. And we have lots of books available for kids who are still gathering information. In researcher's workshop, kids work independently on a variety of nonfiction tasks and projects.

TEACHING MOVES	**TEACHING LANGUAGE**

Connect and Engage

Review how to make a poster and introduce other ways to share learning— making a poem or a book.

Here's my poster—remember it? It's about the katydid. *[I retrieve the poster I made in Lesson 21.]* Let's review. I drew and labeled my picture and put my Post-its on it. I put all my learning about the katydid on this big piece of paper. We're going to keep doing research today in our researcher's workshop, but we're also going to learn more ways to make our learning visible so that we can share it! Just look around the classroom at all this great work you have been doing; you are just exploding with great thinking and learning!

We'll focus on three ways to summarize and synthesize our learning: creating a poster, a poem, or a book. Let's start by reviewing what Briana did to create a poster.

Create a Poster

Review making a poster using a child's example or using the poster modeled in Lesson 21.

Briana did a great job of organizing her thinking about the jaguar on a poster. Would you share what you did, Briana?

> Briana: I put my "I wonders" first—these are blue Post-its. I said, "I wonder if jaguars live in trees" and "I wonder if jaguars eat meat." Then I found my answers. I learned they eat three-toed sloths, so they eat meat. I learned they live in trees, so I drew an arrow from that question to my answer. I also drew a square and drew a picture of a jaguar in a tree. I learned that jaguars are six-feet long, so I wrote an L and drew a picture of a jaguar next to a person lying down; they are the same size! I learned some more stuff and drew a big picture of a jaguar. Then I added my poem on the poster.

TIP: We demonstrate how to think through and create a poster using a child's example to send the message that all kids can make a great poster. If you don't have children's work available, create your own or use the poster from Lesson 21.

Wow, Briana! You've synthesized your learning and included a poem, all on one poster. Notice how Briana's writing and illustrations help her reader understand the information she is sharing. Be sure to take plenty of time to carefully illustrate the information you share. I think Briana drew a picture for

TEACHING LANGUAGE　　　　　　　　　　**TEACHING MOVES**

every fact she included. She illustrated the information that "jaguars hunt at night" with a picture of a jaguar hunting under the stars. We can learn so much when we view and read the information on your poster, Briana.

Also think about visual and text features you can put on your poster that will help your reader understand the information. Briana's comparison of a jaguar next to a six-foot-tall person helps us visualize so we understand how long jaguars are. I've seen many of you use other features on your posters—close-ups, maps, etc. If any of you are wondering what features to include on your poster, check out some of the posters already hanging up.

TIP: Posters allow kids to literally and visually put all their thinking together—providing a concrete way to get across to them what it means to synthesize learning.

Model and Guide

Now let's think about another way to share our learning—by creating a poem.

Model writing poetry as one way to synthesize and share new learning.

TIP: We model options for creating posters, poetry, and books over several days, creating these products ourselves. We also use kids' completed examples as models.

Model and share words that describe visual images and sounds.

TIP: Brainstorming poetic language gets kids "in the mood" for poetry. We write this language on informal word charts shown here.

Create a Poem

When we write poetry, we play with words, visualize, and use vivid language to bring the rain forest's sights and sounds to life! We create mind pictures and then we can write words that describe these.

Think about how some of the rain forest animals move. Do you remember the boa constrictor in *The Great Kapok Tree?* Think about the beautiful language in that story. I have a picture in my mind of that very green snake slithering silently through huge green leaves. I could write about that.

Let's think about how other animals move. Insects and birds fly and flap around the trees. Here are some words that describe flying: *soaring, dipping, swooping, plunging.* Let's act them out. Stand up and *soar!* How does a harpy eagle soar? Way up in the sky above the trees! And then let's *swoop* and *plunge.* *[I write words that describe flying on the chart.]*

How does the rain forest sound? Turn and talk—but instead of talking, see if you can *buzz,* or *chirp,* or *howl,* or make another sound of the rain forest. *[Kids have fun making rain forest sounds. Then they call out the sounds they were making.]* I'll write these words on our *Rain Forest Poetry* word chart. When you write your own poem, you can look at the charts for descriptive language and how to spell words.

Let's begin writing a poem together. Imagine we are in the middle of the hot, sticky rain forest and we see a harpy eagle high in the sky. I'll start writing a poem about the soaring harpy eagle. *[I compose the poem out loud—writing it on the chart.]* Now you can try playing with words to write your own poem! You can use the words on our charts or any others that describe life in the rain forest.

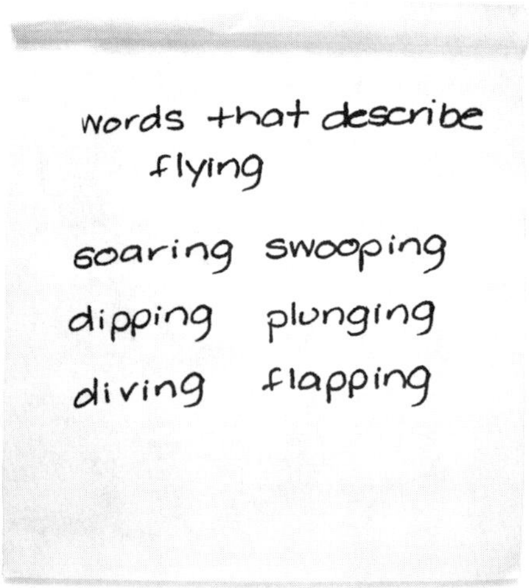

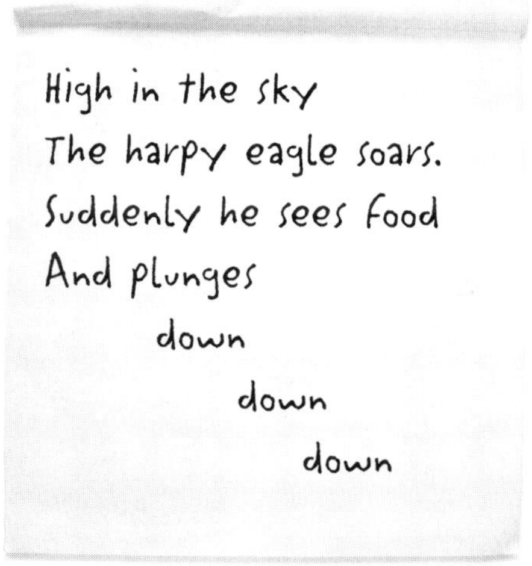

words that describe
flying

soaring   swooping
dipping   plunging
diving   flapping

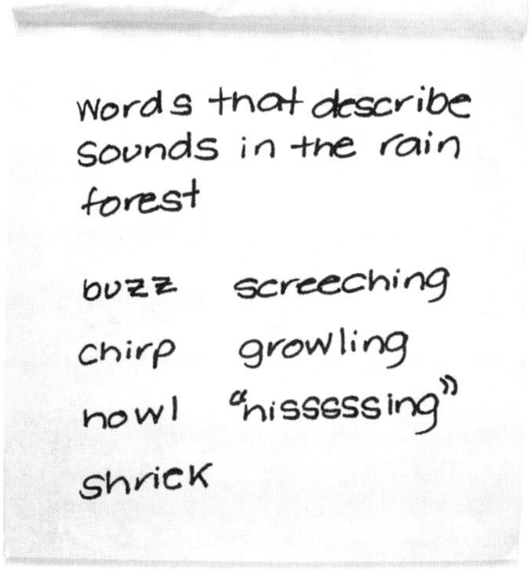

Words that describe
sounds in the rain
forest

buzz   screeching
chirp   growling
howl   "hissessing"
shriek

High in the sky
The harpy eagle soars.
Suddenly he sees food
And plunges
    down
       down
          down

Create a Book

Another option is to *write a book*, which is similar to the teaching books you've already written (Lesson 5). These books are different, because you are writing about your research and all the information you have learned. You'll want to write the title—what the book is about—on the cover page. Then you can use the information you've researched to write important and interesting information about your topic on the rest of the pages. I'll read a few pages of my book on the red-eyed tree frog.

Here's my book. I started writing it earlier so I could show it to you. *[I read.]* Notice that I put one big idea on each page and then added all the information that's connected to that idea. Now I'll draw some illustrations. These will help my information come alive. And last but not least, I'll think about using text and visual features— like these pictures and labels—to help readers learn new and interesting information. If you would like to make a book to share your learning about the rain forest, there is paper right here.

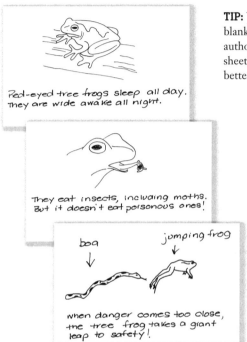

Model how to write and illustrate a book, another way to synthesize and share new knowledge.

TIP: We can quickly make a blank book for our would-be authors by folding and stapling sheets of 8 1/2 x 11 or, even better, 11 x 17 paper.

Collaborate or Practice Independently

You're going to choose what you will do during researcher's workshop. Many of you are already reading, writing, and researching in all the ways we've been talking about. And now we have some more choices for projects you can create to share your learning. Have fun!

[I confer with kids as they work, guiding them to organize their thinking, supporting them to create a poster or write a poem, or helping them write a self-published book. I ask a couple of kids to share their work during the forthcoming sharing circle and rehearse with them what they will say to the group.]

Give kids options for doing research: reading, writing, and thinking about information or working on a project to synthesize their learning.

TIP: Practicing how they will share their learning helps kids focus on what they want to share and keep their audience in mind.

Share the Learning

You all have found so many amazing ways to share what you have been learning in our researcher's workshop. I've asked Jeremiah to start our sharing today. We are going to listen to and think about the information about bats that Jeremiah has discovered and synthesized. I know many of you are interested in this topic because I've heard you talking with Jeremiah as he worked on his bat poster.

Ask kids to share their poems, posters, and books.

Teach kids ways to respond to and discuss their peers' projects.

TIP: We encourage kids to go beyond polite comments about one another's work to asking questions, sharing their own knowledge, or responding to specific information. In this way, sharing time provides many opportunities for teaching and learning.

TIP: In Active Literacy Classrooms, kids share their learning with teachers, parents, librarians, and principals, as well as with kids. We make sure all the adults in our learning community feel welcome.

Invite kids to respond through writing and drawing and adding comments to their classmates' work.

"I can't believe the flying fox only eats fruit!"

After Jeremiah shares what he has learned, I'm going to ask you all to participate. When Jeremiah is done, he will ask if you have questions, comments, or connections. That will be your cue to turn and talk about something you learned from or wondered about Jeremiah's presentation. So, as he shares, think about a question that pops into your mind or a connection you have to this topic. You are also welcome to make positive comments—noticing the interesting pictures Jeremiah drew or commenting on some amazing information you learned from him.

Zoe: We can say, "We like your research about bats."

Exactly, Zoe, but you might also add why you liked Jeremiah's research or what was particularly interesting about it. Be specific about why you liked the research or what you learned from it, OK? There are lots of possible responses. Let's try it.

[Jeremiah presents his bat research and shows his poster.]

Jeremiah: Any questions, comments, or connections? Kiel, would you like to share?

Kiel: Yes, thank you. I was wondering—Do vampire bats bite humans?

Jeremiah: I don't think so, but I have these books here and you could look in one of those to find out.

Great suggestion.

Jeremiah: Any other comments, questions, or connections?

[Kids raise their hands. Jeremiah calls on Bergen, and the discussion continues.]

Bergen: Do bats bite other bats?

Jeremiah: I don't know. I know they eat fruit, but we could check.

Miguel: I love your research. How did you get the idea to research bats?

Jeremiah: I saw a photograph of a fruit bat, and I wondered if other bats lived in the rain forest. So I started reading about bats.

Jean (another classroom teacher): I was surprised to learn that bats have five toes.

Jeremiah: And they are mammals, like us!

You have such thoughtful comments and questions. Now, I'd like each of you to write a response to Jeremiah's poster—a connection, a question, or a comment—on a Post-it. *[I hand out Post-its and pencils.]* You can write your thoughts in words and draw pictures, too. Then, if it's OK with Jeremiah, we'll put all your great thinking around his poster. *[Kids write and draw their responses, and then put them on the bat poster.]*

Let's keep going. We'll share more comments as each of you presents. When you teach all of us about your research, we learn so much from one another!

Did your students:

■ summarize and synthesize what they learned by making posters, poems, books, and other projects?

■ share new knowledge and teach it to their peers and teachers?

■ participate in a community of researchers by thoughtfully responding to each other's projects?

Reflect& Assess

Kids create original projects when given the support and time to work independently. As they become more self-reliant, we give them more time to work on projects. In this way, kids can synthesize learning—"putting it all together." We take a broad view of synthesis—a synthesis can be a short poem or a large poster that kids return to over time. What's important is that kids are adding to their evolving thinking as they learn more about the topic. We assess how kids are synthesizing their learning through individual conferences, and we continue to teach as kids create projects. We try to keep the big picture in mind: Are kids organizing their thinking and creating ways to share their learning? Can they articulate the process they used to create a poster, poem, or book? Are they responding to each other's work respectfully and thoughtfully?

Adapt& Differentiate

This lesson was done with first graders, but here are suggestions for how to adapt and differentiate with the whole range of learners.

The researcher's workshop is inherently differentiated. Kids' projects illustrate the diverse thinking that occurs when they begin to share ideas for projects with each other. Projects are geared to kids' reading/writing development. Kindergarteners often work in groups to paint a picture of what they are researching. Then they add labels or a sentence strip with a bit of information that describes the picture. (See the Content Literacy slide show for additional examples of research in kindergarten.) We also script young children's language—and they draw the pictures, as Natasha does in her poem about tigers (page 57). More developed readers and writers enjoy the independence that researcher's workshop fosters. Once kids have internalized ways to read, think, and write about their learning, they use these strategies as tools. This workshop format is one of the best ways we know of to accommodate a wide range of learners. Each child can work at his or her own pace on a project of his or her own choosing.

This poster about snakes originated with two Post-its and expanded from there. Ezekiel collected his questions and the facts he learned on a large piece of paper and added to it during the classroom researcher's workshop. He worked on his poster over many weeks, dispelling any notions that kids get "tired" of topics after a while. His engagement and interest deepened as his knowledge of snakes grew by leaps and bounds.

Poetry   Poems can be very simple. I look for free verse, vivid language, an unusual perspective, and detailed illustrations that complement the poem's words and ideas.

This young child wanted to type her poem, so I helped her type it and print it out. Then she illustrated it, although her words are far more graphic than her drawing!

This student loves spiders and could hardly wait to write about them. We discussed adding a bit of action to the poem, which he did in his illustration. A Post-it response from a peer says, "I wonder if spiders live in the rain forest."

August's poem about the eating behaviors of piranhas demonstrates how kids take ideas from the minilesson to create a poem.

Two children—Jacob and Laura—created this book about the parts of the butterfly. They followed the teaching point that each page should include one big idea as well as illustrations and features that elucidate that idea.

The tongue is like a straw
It sucks up nectar.

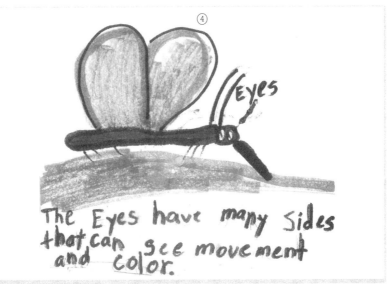

The Eyes have many sides
that can see movement
and color.

The butterfly uses It's two
Antennae to smell.

Share Your Learning

Create projects to demonstrate understanding

TEACHING MOVES	TEACHING LANGUAGE
	Connect and Engage
Review how to make a poster and introduce other ways to share learning—making a poem or a book.	■ We're going to learn ways to share our learning as we create posters, poems, and books. In this way, we can summarize and synthesize our learning.
Review making a poster using a child's example or using the poster modeled in Lesson 21.	■ …did a great job organizing some thinking about…on a poster. Would you share what you did…?
	■ Notice how…'s illustrations help the reader understand the information…visual and text features make the poster information interesting and engaging…and that you can organize and put all your information together in ways that make sense to the reader. Remember, that's what we call *synthesizing!*
	Model and Guide
Model writing poetry as one way to synthesize and share new learning.	■ Another way we can synthesize our learning is through poetry. When we write poetry, we play with words and create mind pictures. We visualize and then write words that describe that picture.
Model and share words that describe visual images and sounds.	■ Let's think about our topic. What are your mind pictures like? What things are happening or moving? Let's act it out. Stand up and bring your ideas alive!
	■ What do you hear? What are some words you can use to describe what you hear? Good! Let me write this down. Who's got more words? You can use the words on the charts and others you think of to create a poem!
Model how to write and illustrate a book, another way to synthesize and share new knowledge.	■ You've already written teaching books on topics you are a specialist in…now you'll want to write important and interesting information, and you'll want to create engaging pictures to go with it.
	■ I have started writing my own book about…. See how I put one big idea on each page? Now I can add some illustrations to make this information come alive for my readers.
	■ If you want to write a book, I can help you make a blank book.

The Teaching Moves outline your instructional sequence and the
Teaching Language gives you an idea about what to say to your students.

TEACHING LANGUAGE	TEACHING MOVES
Collaborate or Practice Independently	
▪ You have lots of choices for what to do during researcher's workshop. You can continue to read, write, and research in the ways we have been talking about, or you can choose to create a poster, poem, or book. Feel free to work by yourself, with a partner, or with a small group.	Give kids options for doing research: reading, writing, and thinking about information or working on a project to synthesize their learning.
Share the Learning	
▪ I've asked…to talk to us about research today. We are going to listen to and think about the information about…that…will be sharing.	Ask kids to share their poems, posters, and books.
▪ When…is finished presenting, you can offer questions, comments, or connections. Be specific about why you liked the research or what you learned from it. Let's try it.	Teach kids ways to respond to and discuss their peers' projects.
▪ Now, I'd like each of you to write or draw a response on a Post-it. If it is OK with…, you can put your Post-its up around the poster.	Invite kids to respond through writing and drawing and adding comments to their classmates' work.
▪ Let's keep sharing. We'll make time for comments as each of you presents, and we'll also write our responses and post them around your projects.	

Reflect & Assess

Did your students:

▪ summarize and synthesize what they learned by making posters, poems, books, and other projects?

▪ share new knowledge and teach it to their peers and teachers?

▪ participate in a community of researchers by thoughtfully responding to each other's projects?

Summarize and Synthesize Strategy Wrap-up:
Creating an Anchor Chart to Capture What We Learned about Summarizing and Synthesizing

Teaching Language

Now that we have done some lessons on synthesizing and summarizing when we read, let's take a look back at what we have learned. We can co-construct an Anchor Chart about this strategy that will serve as a visual reminder to help us pull out the most important information, issues, or ideas. You have such great ideas for sharing your work and thinking. Let's get some of these up on our Anchor Chart.

I'll begin by sharing something I do when I synthesize information and I will record it on the chart. For instance, when I'm trying to synthesize information, I have to stop and think about the bits of information as I read to come up with the big picture. While I am jotting this down on the chart, turn to each other and talk. Tell something you have learned about synthesizing information that we need to think about when we read, write, and draw. Be sure to say it in a way that makes sense to you.

[Kids turn and talk.]

Let's share some of your thoughts.

[We want to capture kids' comments that show their understanding of the strategy as well as our lesson language to guide future teaching and learning.]

What We Learned about Summarizing and Synthesizing

We stop and think while we read, gathering up bits of information to come up with the big picture.

We put the information into our own words to show that we understand it.

We don't tell too much.

We show our understanding of information and big ideas through talking, writing, and drawing.

We create many different ways to show what we have learned and share it with others. We make our thinking visible through poems, books, posters, reports, plays, and anything else we think of!

We listen carefully to our friends as they share their learning with us. Then we respond with comments and questions.

We draw and write our responses and add them to our friends' work.

Assessment Checklist for Summarize and Synthesize

Expectations for student thinking and learning

- Put the information into one's own words to demonstrate understanding
- Summarize by telling what's important without telling too much
- Stop and think to synthesize the information as they go
- Summarize and synthesize learning through writing and drawing
- Engage in reading, writing, and research using a variety of comprehension strategies
- Create a variety of projects that demonstrate understanding and teach what one has learned to others

---

Questions you can ask yourself to assess student understanding

- Are students able to paraphrase, to put the information into their own words?
- Can they summarize information succinctly and accurately?
- Do they use a variety of strategies to understand big ideas and focus in on important information?
- Can students pull together what they have learned to share it— making thinking and learning visible through drawing, writing, talking?
- Are students interested in teaching others and learning from others? Do they eagerly participate in the classroom learning community?

Language of summarizing and synthesizing

"I never knew…Now I know"

"Aha!…"

"Now I get it…"

"I think the big idea is…"

"I think what's important is…"

"This is what I think…what do you think?"

Comments in response to other learners sharing their work

"Tell me more about…"

"I wonder, how did you…or why did you…?"

"I have a comment…"

"I have a connection…"

"I have a question…"

"I have a compliment… I like how you…"

Annotated Rubric for Strategy Book 6:
Summarize and Synthesize

Name _____ *Date* _____

Oral and/or Written Evidence	Strong Evidence 3		Some Evidence 2		Little Evidence 1
Merges thinking (questions, connections, inferences) to understand important information and surface key ideas					
Puts information into own words without saying too much					
Synthesizes big ideas from a collection of facts					
Creates ways to write, draw, and share learning and make thinking visible					
Responds to and learns from peers and participates in a community of learners					

© 2008 by Stephanie Harvey and Anne Goudvis from *The Primary Comprehension Toolkit*
Portsmouth, NH: Heinemann. This page may be photocopied for classroom use only.

Name _____ Date _____

© 2008 by Stephanie Harvey and Anne Goudvis from *The Primary Comprehension Toolkit*
Portsmouth, NH: Heinemann. This page may be photocopied for classroom use only.

Name _____   Date _____

© 2008 by Stephanie Harvey and Anne Goudvis from *The Primary Comprehension Toolkit*
Portsmouth, NH: Heinemann. This page may be photocopied for classroom use only.